My First Holy Communion
Prayer Book & Journal

by Mary B

My First Holy Communion
Prayer Book & Journal

Name:

Date of Ceremony: ....

Place: ....

Time: ....

Prayer Index

Sign of the Cross

In the name of
the Father,
and of the Son,
and of the
Holy Spirit.

Amen

Morning Prayer

God, our Father,
I offer you today,
all that I think and do,
and say. I offer it with
what was done on earth
by Jesus Christ,
your Son.

Amen

Hail Mary

Hail Mary, full of grace,
the Lord is with thee.
Blessed art thou among
women, and blessed is
the fruit of thy womb
Jesus. Holy Mary, Mother
of God, pray for us sinners,
now, and at the hour
of our death.

Amen

Glory Be to the Father

Glory Be to the
Father, and to the
Son, and to the
Holy Spirit: As it was
in the beginning, is now
and ever shall be,
world without end.

Amen

Act of Contrition

My God, I am sorry for my
sins with all my heart.
In choosing to do wrong,
and failing to do good, I have
sinned against you whom I
should love above all things.
I firmly intend, with your help,
to do penance, to sin no more,
and to avoid whatever leads
me to sin. Our Savior,
Jesus Christ, suffered and
died for us. In his name,
my God, have mercy.

Our Father

Our Father, who art
in heaven, hallowed be
thy name. Thy kingdom come,
thy will be done on earth
as it is in heaven. Give us
this day our daily bread,
and forgive us our
trespasses as we forgive
those who trespass against
us, and lead us not into
temptation, but
deliver us from evil.
Amen

Act of Consecration to Mary

O my Queen, O my
Mother, I love you and
give myself to you.
I give to you this day
my eyes, my ears, my
mouth, my heart, my
whole self. Since I am
yours help me as
your child forever.

Amen

Grace Before Meals

Bless us, O Lord,
and these, thy
gifts, which we
are about to receve
from Thy Bounty.
Through Christ
our Lord.

Amen

Grace After Meals

We give thee
thanks Almighty God
for all thy gifts
which we have
received from
thy goodness,
through Christ
our Lord.

Amen

Prayer to the
Guardian Angel

Angel of God, my
guardian dear, to whom
God's love commits me
here. Ever this day
be at my side,
to light and guard,
to rule and guide.

Amen

My Personal Prayers

My Personal Prayers

My Personal Prayers

My Personal Prayers

My Personal Prayers

My Personal Prayers

My Personal Prayers

My Personal Prayers

My Personal Prayers

My Personal Prayers

My Personal Prayers

My Personal Prayers

My Personal Prayers

My Personal Prayers

My Personal Prayers

My Personal Prayers

My Personal Prayers

My Personal Prayers

My Personal Prayers

My Personal Prayers

Prayers for Family & Friends

_____

_____

_____

_____

_____

_____

_____

_____

_____

_____

Draw a Picture

Prayers for Family & Friends

_____
_____
_____
_____
_____
_____
_____
_____
_____
_____

Draw a Picture

Prayers for Family & Friends

_____
_____
_____
_____
_____
_____
_____
_____
_____

Draw a Picture

Prayers for Family & Friends

_____

_____

_____

_____

_____

_____

_____

_____

_____

Draw a Picture

Prayers for Family & Friends

_____
_____
_____
_____
_____
_____
_____
_____
_____
_____

Draw a Picture

Prayers for Family & Friends

_____

_____

_____

_____

_____

_____

_____

_____

_____

_____

_____

Draw a Picture

Prayers for Family & Friends

_____
_____
_____
_____
_____
_____
_____
_____
_____

Draw a Picture

Prayers for Family & Friends

_____

_____

_____

_____

_____

_____

_____

_____

_____

_____

_____

Draw a Picture

Prayers for Family & Friends

_____

_____

_____

_____

_____

_____

_____

_____

_____

_____

Draw a Picture

Prayers for Family & Friends

Draw a Picture

Prayers for
Family & Friends

Draw a Picture

Prayers for Family & Friends

_____

_____

_____

_____

_____

_____

_____

_____

_____

_____

Draw a Picture

Prayers for Family & Friends

_____
_____
_____
_____
_____
_____
_____
_____
_____
_____

Draw a Picture

Prayers for Family & Friends

_____
_____
_____
_____
_____
_____
_____
_____
_____
_____
_____

Draw a Picture

Prayers for Family & Friends

_____

_____

_____

_____

_____

_____

_____

_____

_____

Draw a Picture

Prayers for Family & Friends

_____

_____

_____

_____

_____

_____

_____

_____

_____

_____

Draw a Picture

Prayers for Family & Friends

Draw a Picture

Prayers for Family & Friends

_____
_____
_____
_____
_____
_____
_____
_____
_____
_____

Draw a Picture

Prayers for Family & Friends

Draw a Picture

Prayers for Family & Friends

_____
_____
_____
_____
_____
_____
_____
_____
_____
_____
_____

Draw a Picture

GRATITUDE JOURNAL

Date:_____

All of the great things in my
life I thank God for today

GRATITUDE JOURNAL

Date:_____

All of the great things in my
life I thank God for today

GRATITUDE JOURNAL

Date:_____

All of the great things in my
life I thank God for today

GRATITUDE JOURNAL

Date:_____

All of the great things in my
life I thank God for today

_____

_____

_____

_____

_____

_____

_____

_____

_____

_____

GRATITUDE JOURNAL

Date:_____

All of the great things in my
life I thank God for today

_____

_____

_____

_____

_____

_____

_____

_____

_____

_____

GRATITUDE JOURNAL

Date:_____

All of the great things in my
life I thank God for today

_____

_____

_____

_____

_____

_____

_____

_____

_____

GRATITUDE JOURNAL

Date:_____

All of the great things in my
life I thank God for today

_____

_____

_____

_____

_____

_____

_____

_____

_____

_____

GRATITUDE JOURNAL

Date:_____

All of the great things in my
life I thank God for today

_____

_____

_____

_____

_____

_____

_____

_____

_____

GRATITUDE JOURNAL

Date:_____

All of the great things in my
life I thank God for today

_____

_____

_____

_____

_____

_____

_____

_____

_____

_____

GRATITUDE JOURNAL

Date:_____

All of the great things in my
life I thank God for today

_____

_____

_____

_____

_____

_____

_____

_____

_____

GRATITUDE JOURNAL

Date:_____

All of the great things in my
life I thank God for today

_____

_____

_____

_____

_____

_____

_____

_____

_____

_____

GRATITUDE JOURNAL

Date:_____

All of the great things in my
life I thank God for today

GRATITUDE JOURNAL

Date:_____

All of the great things in my
life I thank God for today

GRATITUDE JOURNAL

Date:_____

All of the great things in my
life I thank God for today

GRATITUDE JOURNAL

Date:_____

All of the great things in my
life I thank God for today

GRATITUDE JOURNAL

Date:_____

All of the great things in my
life I thank God for today

_____

_____

_____

_____

_____

_____

_____

_____

_____

GRATITUDE JOURNAL

Date:_____

All of the great things in my
life I thank God for today

GRATITUDE JOURNAL

Date:_____

All of the great things in my
life I thank God for today

_____

_____

_____

_____

_____

_____

_____

_____

_____

GRATITUDE JOURNAL

Date:_____

All of the great things in my
life I thank God for today

GRATITUDE JOURNAL

Date:_____

All of the great things in my
life I thank God for today

_____

_____

_____

_____

_____

_____

_____

_____

_____

_____

GRATITUDE JOURNAL

Date:_____

All of the great things in my
life I thank God for today

GRATITUDE JOURNAL

Date:_____

All of the great things in my
life I thank God for today

GRATITUDE JOURNAL

Date:_____

All of the great things in my
life I thank God for today

GRATITUDE JOURNAL

Date:_____

All of the great things in my
life I thank God for today

_____

_____

_____

_____

_____

_____

_____

_____

GRATITUDE JOURNAL

Date:_____

All of the great things in my
life I thank God for today

GRATITUDE JOURNAL

Date:_____

All of the great things in my
life I thank God for today

GRATITUDE JOURNAL

Date:_____

All of the great things in my
life I thank God for today

GRATITUDE JOURNAL

Date:_____

All of the great things in my
life I thank God for today

_____

_____

_____

_____

_____

_____

_____

_____

_____

_____

GRATITUDE JOURNAL

Date:_____

All of the great things in my
life I thank God for today

GRATITUDE JOURNAL

Date:_____

All of the great things in my
life I thank God for today

My First Holy Communion
JOURNAL

My First Holy Communion
JOURNAL

My First Holy Communion
JOURNAL

My First Holy Communion
JOURNAL

My First Holy Communion
JOURNAL

My First Holy Communion
JOURNAL

My First Holy Communion
JOURNAL

My First Holy Communion
JOURNAL

My First Holy Communion
JOURNAL

My First Holy Communion
JOURNAL

My First Holy Communion
JOURNAL

My First Holy Communion
JOURNAL

My First Holy Communion
JOURNAL

My First Holy Communion
JOURNAL

My First Holy Communion
JOURNAL

My First Holy Communion
JOURNAL

My First Holy Communion
JOURNAL

My First Holy Communion
JOURNAL

My First Holy Communion
JOURNAL

My First Holy Communion
JOURNAL

My First Holy Communion
JOURNAL

My First Holy Communion
JOURNAL

My First Holy Communion
JOURNAL

My First Holy Communion
JOURNAL

My First Holy Communion
JOURNAL

My First Holy Communion
JOURNAL

My First Holy Communion
JOURNAL

My First Holy Communion
JOURNAL

My First Holy Communion
JOURNAL

My First Holy Communion
JOURNAL

My First Holy Communion
JOURNAL

My First Holy Communion
JOURNAL

My First Holy Communion
JOURNAL

My First Holy Communion
JOURNAL

My First Holy Communion
JOURNAL

My First Holy Communion
JOURNAL

My First Holy Communion
JOURNAL

My First Holy Communion
JOURNAL

My First Holy Communion
JOURNAL

My First Holy Communion
JOURNAL

Made in the USA
Middletown, DE
20 July 2022